Wise Words from

Change
Makers

Harper *by* Design

In 1921, Edith Cowan became Australia's first female parliamentarian, following her instrumental work in securing the right to vote for women in Western Australia.

In 1955, Rosa Parks, a seamstress at a local Alabama department store, rejected an order from a bus driver to vacate her seat in favour of a white passenger. Her small act of defiance would inspire millions of Black Americans fighting against segregation and earn her the title of 'the first lady of civil rights' as bestowed by the US Congress.

In 2018, Swedish teenager Greta Thunberg camped outside Parliament in Stockholm with a simple sign calling for stronger action on climate change. She is now considered one of the world's leading activists, is the youngest ever *Time* Person of the Year and has been nominated for the Nobel Peace Prize three times.

Change makers are all around us. Empathetic, curious, courageous, entrepreneurial and often relentless, they identify social or ethical problems and use creative action to solve them. They see the beauty and positivity in the world, and believe in a bright future. They don't believe in problems, but in possibilities.

That spirit is reflected in this collection of popular quotes from a variety of global change makers who have helped shift the conversation forward in some way, shape or form. We salute them for the great work they do.

Rights are won only
by those who make their
voices heard.

HARVEY MILK

We deserve to experience love fully, equally, without shame and without compromise.

ELLIOT PAGE

You always learn a lot
more when you lose.

ASH BARTY

Confidence is sexy.

JONATHAN VAN NESS

Do one thing every day
that scares you.

ELEANOR ROOSEVELT

What keeps me motivated to keep going is, when you look back, you can see that you are constantly moving forward. It doesn't feel like that at the time, but you are.

ROSIE BATTY

14

We need both facts
and poetry in our lives.
Sometimes facts can tell
truth better than poetry,
and sometimes poetry can
tell truth better than facts.

CHLOÉ ZHAO

What I am absolutely confident of is it will be easier for the next woman and the woman after that and the woman after that. And I'm proud of that.

JULIA GILLARD

Revolutions that last
don't happen from the
top down. They happen
from the bottom up.

GLORIA STEINEM

I refuse to believe that
you cannot be both
compassionate and strong.

JACINDA ARDERN

Be open to new ideas and experiences because you'll never know when someone else will have an interesting thought or when a new door will open to take you on the journey of your dreams.

KETANJI BROWN JACKSON

25

Darkness cannot drive out darkness; only light can do that. Hate cannot drive out hate; only love can do that.

MARTIN LUTHER KING JR.

Your self-worth is
determined by you.
You don't have to depend
on someone telling you
who you are.

BEYONCÉ

I've learnt that no one
is too small to make
a difference.

GRETA THUNBERG

Owning up to your
vulnerabilities is
a form of strength.

LIZZO

Inherently, having privilege isn't bad, but it's how you use it, and you have to use it in service of other people.

TARANA BURKE

I believe whenever you're trying something new, it's always going to get some kind of bad reception.

LIL NAS X

Real change, enduring
change, happens one
step at a time.

RUTH BADER GINSBURG

I do like to think of myself as a star: because there's room for many stars up in the sky — and we all have the chance to shine bright.

MJ RODRIGUEZ

I always believed that
when you follow your
heart or your gut you
can never lose, because
settling is the worst
feeling in the world.

RIHANNA

Listen, just go out into the world and try everything.

KYLIE KWONG

There is always light.
If only we're brave
enough to see it.
If only we're brave
enough to be it.

AMANDA GORMAN

46

It is better to inspire
a reform than to
enforce it.

CATHERINE THE GREAT

Never accept compromise on your standards – always aim to be the best you can be in whatever you do.

JENNY KEE

50

I believe there is only one race – the human race.

ROSA PARKS

In the end, I still believe there is no greater joy than sharing food, conversation and laughter around a table.

STEPHANIE ALEXANDER

If they don't give you a
seat at the table, bring
a folding chair.

SHIRLEY CHISHOLM

People get into politics
to make change, to
give back, to add value.
Politics isn't the only
way you can do that.

ANNE ALY

Though the sex to
which I belong is
considered weak you
will nevertheless find
me a rock that bends
to no wind.

QUEEN ELIZABETH I

A lot of times, the people who have the confidence to say, "I don't know what the rules are, so I'm just going to do what I want" are the most exciting people.

DANIEL KALUUYA

I feel like it's actually everybody's responsibility to use whatever platform they have to do good in the world, and to try make our society better.

MEGAN RAPINOE

I think women are
very powerful and I think
we're more powerful
together than separated.

ZENDAYA

We need to encourage
black women to know
that they are authors
of their own destiny.

MICHAELA COEL

My love is political.
My body is political. I talk
even when I don't speak.

INDYA MOORE

I'm not setting too many expectations for myself. I'm just trying to create opportunities for something interesting.

BOWEN YANG

If you're always trying
to be normal, you
will never know how
amazing you can be.

MAYA ANGELOU

What counts in life is
not the mere fact that
we have lived. It is what
difference we have made
to the lives of others.

NELSON MANDELA

Those who deny freedom
to others, deserve it not
for themselves.

ABRAHAM LINCOLN

What an amazing gift
to help people, not
just yourself.

BARACK OBAMA

You have to believe
in yourself when no
one else does.

SERENA WILLIAMS

I want to raise men
to the level of women.

EDITH COWAN

I think it's just as important what you say no to as what you say yes to.

SANDRA OH

We all need to be the
role models we needed
when we were growing up.

BENJAMIN LAW

Be less curious about people and more curious about ideas.

MARIE CURIE

I don't want a cure for my disability, I want a cure for other people's ableism.

CARLY FINDLAY

Sometimes defiance is all we have.

STAN GRANT

Harper *by* Design
An imprint of HarperCollins*Publishers*

HarperCollins*Publishers*
Australia • Brazil • Canada • France • Germany • Holland • India
Italy • Japan • Mexico • New Zealand • Poland • Spain • Sweden
Switzerland • United Kingdom • United States of America

HarperCollins acknowledges the Traditional Custodians of the land upon which we live and work, and pays respect to Elders past and present.

First published in Australia in 2022
by HarperCollins*Publishers* Australia Pty Limited
Gadigal Country
Level 13, 201 Elizabeth Street, Sydney NSW 2000
ABN 36 009 913 517
harpercollins.com.au

A catalogue record for this book is available from the National Library of Australia

ISBN 978 1 4607 6264 6

Publisher: Mark Campbell
Publishing Director: Brigitta Doyle
Project Editor: Hella Ibrahim
Designer: Mietta Yans, HarperCollins Design Studio
Illustrator: Sol Cotti
Quote page 54 by Stephanie Alexander from her book *Home* published by Pan Macmillan, 2021
Colour reproduction by Splitting Image Colour Studio, Clayton VIC
Printed and bound in China by RR Donnelley

8 7 6 5 4 3 2 1   22 23 24 25